BOA CON

A

Every Detailed Guide On Boa Constrictors Care, Feeding, Housing, Diet And Health Care

Dr. Crassus Cup

Table of Contents

CHAPTER ONE 4

  BOA CONSTRICTORS 4

  BOA CONSTRICTORS FOOD 6

CHAPTER TWO 8

  BOA CONSTRICTORS FEEDING 8

  BOA CONSTRICTORS HANDLING 9

  BOA CONSTRICTOR BEHAVIOR AND TEMPERAMENT..10

  BOA CONSTRICTORS HOUSING 11

CHAPTER THREE 14

  BOA CONSTRICTORS HEAT 14

  LIGHT..16

  HUMIDITY 16

  SUBSTRATE..17

CHAPTER FOUR 19

  BOA CONSTRICTORS FOOD AND WATER 19

  BOA CONSTRICTORS HEALTH AND BEHAVIOR PROBLEMS 21

THE END 23

CHAPTER ONE

BOA CONSTRICTORS

Boa constrictor thrives in tropical rainforests; it also inhabits savannas, cane fields, and semiarid scrublands. The snake's adult length is usually about 10 feet (3 metres), though individuals of quite 18 feet (5.5 metres). The amount of Constrictor subspecies is disputed, starting from 6 to 11. The head of the Constrictor is long and triangular, with dark streaks from the eyes to the rear of the jaw and another dark streak along the highest.

The essential coloration is deep brown-and-black markings often within the shape of triangles, ovals, and joined ovals against a pale brown-and-gray background. However, colours and markings frequently vary, not only among the subspecies but also among individuals within the same population.

The Constrictor is active from dusk to dawn, feeding on a good sort of birds and mammals. It's mostly terrestrial but climbs into trees in search of birds. In daytime it shelters in tree hollows, old logs, and animal burrows. It kills by constriction, first grasping the prey then using its coils to exert a deadly amount of pressure. Slow moving and of a light temperament, it's easily tamed.

BOA CONSTRICTORS FOOD

In the wild, boa constrictors eat a spread of small animals. Their preferred food is bats, but they also consume large lizards, birds, rats and squirrels. In captivity, boa constrictors are typically fed rodents, although the National Zoo supplements its boas' diets with chicks. Boas within the wild kill their food by constricting around it, but feeding live animals to snakes in captivity is controversial. If your boa doesn't kill a prey animal directly, the animal might fight back and injure the snake. Some snake owners feel that a fast, clean kill is more humane.

CHAPTER TWO

BOA CONSTRICTORS FEEDING

The size of the food should be proportional to the dimensions of the snake. Choose a rodent that's approximately an equivalent girth because the snake. Baby boas typically begin with pinkie mice, which are babies who don't yet have fur, while full-grown adults generally eat large rats. Feed just one prey item at each feeding. Thaw frozen rodents during a zip-top bag submerged in warm, but not hot, water for 15-30 minutes counting on the rodent's size. Use a pair of tongs to present the prey to the snake. Never hand-feed your Constrictor, as your snake could learn to associate your hands with food, resulting in injury.

BOA CONSTRICTORS HANDLING

Do not handle a snake that has recently eaten. Consistent with The Urban Python, boa constrictors need a minimum of 48 hours to properly digest a meal. Provide a dark, sheltered spot within the cage for the snake to twist up out of view, and leave it alone. You'll perform minimal cage maintenance if necessary, but save major tasks for an additional time.

BOA CONSTRICTOR BEHAVIOR AND TEMPERAMENT

Boas are typically active, alert snakes. They could hiss or bite if they feel threatened, but consistent handling usually will make them tame and not so defensive. It's important to understand the way to hold a boa, so it feels secure. One hand should be under its body near its head, and therefore the other hand should be under the rear half its body. The boa might loosely wrap itself around you for added support, but it typically won't constrict unless it feels alarmed or like it's falling.

BOA CONSTRICTORS HOUSING

While baby boa constrictors are often housed in glass aquariums, larger snakes will need a custom enclosure that's either commercially purchased or constructed reception. Boa constrictors are very powerful and can escape if given the prospect , so enclosures must be secure.1 an honest enclosure size for an adult Constrictor constrictor is around 6 to eight feet long, 2 to three feet wide, and a couple of to three feet tall. The minimum size is around 10 square feet of floor space for one snake. Hide boxes are essential to form your snake feel secure. A minimum of two hides should be provided within the enclosure, one at each end of the gradient.

Hides are often half logs, commercial reptile caves, upside-down plastic containers with a hole cut within the side, or maybe cardboard boxes. Confirm they're not much larger than the snake, as an in depth fit will help the snake feel safe. They ought to be cleaned or replaced once they become soiled.

A cleaned and sterilized limb that's heavy enough to support the snake's weight should even be provided within the enclosure. Soak it during a bleach solution, rinse it, and dry it thoroughly before adding it if you bought it from outside. Store-bought driftwood also can be used.

CHAPTER THREE

BOA CONSTRICTORS HEAT

Boa constrictors come from tropical climates, so warm temperatures in their enclosures are essential. During the day, a gradient between 82 to 90 degrees Fahrenheit (28 to 32 degrees Celsius) should be maintained. Also, a basking spot of 90 to 95 degrees Fahrenheit (32 to 35 degrees Celsius) should be provided. At night, temperatures can drop to 78 to 85 degrees Fahrenheit (26 to 30 degrees Celsius).

The temperatures in your snake's cage are critical, so accurate thermometers with measurements in several locations of the enclosure (the warm end, cool end, and basking spot) are a requirement. A mixture of incandescent bulbs, ceramic heating elements, and heating pads are often wont to maintain the temperatures. Any bulbs or heating elements within the enclosure must be shielded to stop burns, to which snakes are quite susceptible. Hot rocks should never be used.

LIGHT

Boas generally don't need any special UV lighting. Their diet should provide them with the vitamin D that they might produce from the sun's UV rays within the wild.

HUMIDITY

Maintain a humidity level within the enclosure of around 60% to 70% Keeping a bowl of water within the enclosure can help to boost the humidity level, alongside misting the world . The snake will likely climb into the water bowl for baths, so confirm it's sturdy and large enough. It should be cleaned regularly, as snakes will often defecate within the water. Shedding snakes can especially enjoy a shower to assist within the natural action.

SUBSTRATE

A variety of materials, or substrates, are often wont to line rock bottom of Constrictor enclosures. The substrate can help to mimic the snake's natural environment, and it'll maintain some humidity. For young snakes, lining the cage with paper or paper towels is usually the simplest option for straightforward cleaning. For adults, paper also can be used, also as reptile carpet. The advantage of carpeting is pieces are often move fit the enclosure and a soiled piece are often replaced with a spare while the soiled piece is cleaned and disinfected. Some owners also use reptile bark, though it is often expensive. Excelsior is best avoided thanks to irritation concerns and therefore the potential for accidental ingestion and impaction.

CHAPTER FOUR

BOA CONSTRICTORS FOOD AND WATER

Young boas should be fed more frequently than adults. Small snakes are often fed every five to seven days, intermediate snakes every 10 to 14 days, and adult snakes every three to four weeks. Adjust feeding to take care of an honest body condition in your snake. And confine mind that a lot of snakes in captivity are overfed, so obesity are often a drag. Hatchling snakes are often fed mice and rabbits (one per feeding) as they grow larger. An adult Constrictor will eat a couple of rats for a meal or one rabbit monthly. Never feed a snake a prey item larger than it's

Moreover, avoid handling your snake for a minimum of 24 hours after a meal, or regurgitation might occur. Boas generally wish to hide with their prey to eat it. So do not be surprised if your snake disappears into a hide box with its meal, and you do not see it for a short time. Feeding time is when the foremost care is required for handling boa constrictors (as with the other snake). don't feed by hand, as this increases the danger of accidental bites if they mistake fingers for food. And wash your hands well after handling food, or the snake might strike at your hand. A handling stick can help to push the snake far away from the cage door at feeding time to stop problems.

BOA CONSTRICTORS HEALTH AND BEHAVIOR PROBLEMS

The most serious disease which will affect boa constrictors is cellular inclusion disease, or IBD.2 this is often a fatal retrovirus that's almost like HIV in humans. An infected snake can appear healthy, because the virus can lay dormant for several years. Symptoms of IBD include boa breathing with its mouth open, poor appetite, and excessive amounts of saliva. In advanced cases, IBD can cause snakes to lose control of their bodily movements.

THE END

Printed in Great Britain
by Amazon